TOYS
MADE OF
ROCK

Bilingual Press/Editorial Bilingüe
Canto Cosas

Series Editor
Francisco Aragón

Publisher
Gary Francisco Keller

Executive Editor
Karen S. Van Hooft

Associate Editor
Linda K. St. George

Address
Bilingual Press
Hispanic Research Center
Arizona State University
PO Box 875303
Tempe, Arizona 85287-5303
(480) 965-3867

José B. González

Bilingual Press/Editorial Bilingüe
TEMPE, ARIZONA

Library of Congress Cataloging-in-Publication Data

González, José B.
   Toys made of rock / José B. González.
      pages   cm. — (Canto cosas)
   Summary: "This volume is a first collection of poems by Salvadoran-born poet, anthologist, and award-winning teacher José B. González. The poems deal with the immigrant experience and issues of identity, resilience, survival, and achievement" — Provided by publisher.
      Text in English and Spanish.
      ISBN 978-1-939743-15-2 (alk. paper)
   1. American poetry—Hispanic American authors. 2. Hispanic American poetry (Spanish) I. González, José B. Poems. Selections. II. González, José B. Poems. Selections. Spanish. III. Title.
   PS3607.O56185A58 2015
   811'.6—dc23

                                       2015018852

PRINTED IN THE UNITED STATES OF AMERICA

Second printing, May 2017

Front cover art: *Lección de vuelo 2* (2015) by Alex Cuchilla
Cover and interior design by John Wincek

Source acknowledgments are found on p. xii.

Canto Cosas

This poetry series, which was initially supported by awards from the National Endowment for the Arts and the Arizona Commission on the Arts, is designed to give further exposure to Latina and Latino poets who have achieved a significant level of critical recognition through individual chapbooks and publication in periodicals or anthologies or both, but who in most cases have not had their own books of poetry published. Under the watchful eye of series editor, poet, and small press publisher Francisco Aragón, the books in Canto Cosas aim to reflect the aesthetic diversity in American poetry. There are no restrictions on ethnicity, nationality, philosophy, ideology, or language; we will simply continue our commitment to producing high-quality poetry. The books in this series will also feature introductions by more established voices in the field.

To those children, the ones with no names,
no homes, no passports, no papers,
and no headlines.

CONTENTS

I

El Salvador

U.S.

Stealing Shakespeare

IV

Classrooms

ACKNOWLEDGMENTS

I would like to thank the many individuals whose love and support during the years it took to compose and eventually publish these poems kept me inspired and made me feel like my words mattered:

Francisco Aragón, padrino of poetry to so many of us; Rhina Espaillat, Mirta Ojito, Brian Turner, and Tino Villanueva, whose willingness to open the pages of this book in manuscript form has meant so much to me; Gary Francisco Keller, Karen Van Hooft, and the rest of the folks at Bilingual Press, whose books have changed the lives of people around the world, including that of a boy growing up in Connecticut who could see himself in their books; and my wife, Kristin, and my children, Cassandra, Olivia, Sofia, and Nolan, who put up with my crankiness after late nights of writing.

Source Acknowledgments

 he following poems (or earlier versions) first appeared in these publications:

"After the Honduras-El Salvador Soccer War of 1969": *Acentos Review.*

"The Art of Flipping": *OCHO.*

"At the Obituary Interview": *Naugatuck River Review.*

"Autobrownography of a New England Latino": *Latino Boom: An Anthology of U.S. Latino Literature*

"Brown University Librarian Strike": *Acentos Review.*

"Caribbean Fresco in New England": *Calabash.*

"City Mouse Chase": *BorderSenses.*

"A Colleague Thinks Ethnic Poetry Is Easy to Write": *The Leaflet.*

"Dark Cinderella": *Quercus Review.*

"Dirtied Gauzes": *Naugatuck River Review.*

"Elvis in the Inner City": *Callaloo: Special Issue on Hip-Hop.*

"Fleeing for Work": *OCHO.*

"Football for the First Time": *OCHO.*

"Hollow Shells Revisited": *Paterson Literary Review.*

"i couldn't for a teenage bully's death": *Acentos Review.*

"In the Company of Books": *Palabra.*

"Letter About Hurricane F—": *Sixers Review.*

"Lines Breaking": *Quercus Review.*

"Lola's Salvadoran Pupusa Stand": *Colere: A Journal of Cultural Exploration.*

"Mami's Days": *Sixers Review.*

"New London Verse": *Sixers Review.*

"Signs of El Salvador": *Melting Trees Review.*

"Sociology 101: Essay on Illegal Immigration": *The Teacher's Voice.*

"Stealing Shakespeare": *Coloring Book.*

"The Thanksgiving of *No Más*": *Palabra.*

"Toys Made of Rock": *Quercus Review.*

DANGEROUS BY DESIGN

THE POETRY OF JOSÉ B. GONZÁLEZ

Rhina P. Espaillat

The title of this first collection by poet, anthologist, and award-winning teacher José B. González is as accurate as it is playful and cruel. Better still, the book fulfills perfectly the difficult, complex promise implied by its title and illustrates how poetry, at its best, can simultaneously delight, wound, and instruct.

As an eight-year-old immigrant from El Salvador, González was already well acquainted with many of the hard, unyielding aspects of a precarious existence: poverty, illness in the family, lack of opportunity, warfare, political corruption, and violence. Those are stony realities, familiar to many of the people who pour into the United States from Latin America and elsewhere in search of something better and then discover that in this land of opportunity the road to achievement is also rocky. Immigrant literature—a rich field in which Latino authors are well represented in every genre—has made those rough roads familiar: the difficulty of learning a new language and new customs; the absence of family and home; the fear of rejection by new neighbors; the feared loss of identity; the doors closed by ignorance, xenophobia, deprivation, and competition. Sometimes those hardships are presented just as they were experienced by the author or by fictional surrogates, other times as heard from family members who came first and forced doors open by dint of sheer persistence, as if to point out that people who survive among rocks can acquire the stubborn endurance of their surroundings and go on to succeed. Sometimes hardship wins, and the newcomer succumbs to a bleak life barely lighted by the hope of something better for the next generation.

Toys Made of Rock confronts all of those themes but is distinctive among such books because the poet has chosen to make out of his raw material not simply history or sociology or politics, but toys. Toys, after all, are instruments of distraction and pleasure, often for children but suitable for everyone, since the desire to look away from the immediate, to play, seems to be a universal and lifelong human trait. What is any art if not a kind of play— a game with surfaces, color, and line, with sound and body gestures, with language, with clay and stone and everything else the world provides? What José González has done is to transform the truths of his largely autobiographical material so that while the matter hurts with its faithful record of losses endured, the manner delights with its appeal to the senses, most especially the ear, and to the intellect through imagery that puts the reader in the skin of the speaker of each poem. The history is here in the details of Salvadoran life in the 1960s, the sociology and politics appear in the various events that illustrate the immigrant's route from stranger to participant in the society, but what draws the reader in is, finally, the unexpected play that makes the trip a dangerous but rewarding pleasure from beginning to end.

The poet accomplishes this by employing all of the devices that prosody offers: rhythm that wanders into and out of regularity, keeping the ear alert to change and flow; rhyme and off-rhyme that winds through poems freely rather than reliably ending his lines; alliteration, echoes, and repetitions that set up a subtle and shifting drumbeat very close to rap. His titles set up expectations that poems then go on to satisfy, but in surprising ways. His approach to the reader shifts from casual news-sharing to intimate confession to direct address that adopts a variety of tones. His figures of speech mine observation and memory to come up with phrases that remain with the reader as if they reflected his or her personal experience. Here are a few examples: In "Tumor Fruit" the father's cancer is explored, traced causally back to the life of the working poor, and finally addressed directly and defiantly: "You eat more than / You're fed, / But I refuse to be dead." The mother, who "sews to sew" her troubled family "whole again," suffers from a "cough of minimum wage." A poem on several of the poet's boyhood friends who are intent on learning "the art of flipping" out of school and work and who died young, went to jail, or otherwise failed, ends with the author's gratitude to Thoreau, who first taught him "the art of flipping book pages." Learning is being held up as the key, but not one to be employed with passive obedience: the classroom experience in its many varieties has taught this poet the importance of ". . . the lonely word, / 'But.' "

A poem that most clearly demonstrates the poet at work transforming life into language is titled "Lines Breaking." It consists of a quarrel with prosody during which the speaker pretends to downplay the value of the very artifices he is employing with casual mastery, and it ends by doing what teachers do: illustrating what works. As a poet, González has clearly learned to use, with a craftsman's joy, everything in the toolbox so as to give each poem access to every device it may choose. As a bilingual immigrant author writing in his second language, González urges his readers (and his students, by implication) to "steal Shakespeare," to appropriate the tradition of any language they can claim, whether by birth or through conscious learning, rather than narrowing their possibilities out of a false sense of loyalty to their own tradition.

Among the many inimitable poems in this collection are "In the Company of Books" and "Arizona Sides," the first forthright in its account of bigotry in action and the second daring in its use of the folk language of bigotry to denounce current bigotry. And "Autobrownography of a New England Latino," perhaps the poet's signature piece, deserves to be read not as an expression of the Latino experience exclusively, but as an utterance of the immigrant everywhere, from any background. It's a poem about identity, its creation by willed accretion, its enrichment by experience, its resilience and importance, and the individual's right to celebrate one's own at every stage of its development.

As a Dominican immigrant in the United States since the age of seven, and, like González, a bilingual author and teacher, not of Spanish but of my second language, I respond to this poem viscerally and always with cheers, especially where the poet describes himself as "master of [his] own / Brown destiny," even on days when he feels as if he's been "brownbeaten." The very humor of the conceit, the assured wordplay, renders the poem an artifact, an intellectual toy, for conveying pleasure in one's own being and for celebrating one's passage through losses and challenges with the capacity to be what one always was, only more so.

What an honor it is to comment on this remarkable book that speaks, with power, grace, and unabashed pride, for the tenacious uprooted who sprout wherever there's a foothold. I'm grateful for the opportunity to congratulate José B. González on it and to wish for the next, and the one after that!

PART

El Salvador

SPANISH ROCKS & ROCKY TOMBS

letter about hurricane f—

dear —:

the winds that sucked
in walls
      & blew
Manito's house
against stones
pushed the *La Prensa* camera
through our front door
& snapped this shot.

white flowers stand on top
of a crucifix & black petals
float around the room as if
the hurricane still breathes.

but the winds can't leave yet.

Tía Lydia needs them
to push her legs
            forward,
so she can walk again,
& i need them
to carry this newspaper
photograph to you.

as you hold it, you'll see
what i mean when i say
i've grown so much
since you left. my head
so close to reaching

the top of the casket.

JOSÉ B. GONZÁLEZ

when he played jesus, walking
the holy week parade miles, circling
trails made of izote flowers, showered
by the prayers of Sonsonate's streets,
his feet would be bare.

mothers would catch up
& drop their change
in front of candles.

his crown would tilt
to the side, slide
on the sweat of his brow. hours
of bowing & hearing
the hollers of miracle seekers
would cloud spots
in his eyes.

skinny children would point
to him, then to a northern star, begging
saints of losses & causes.

as long as they touched
the hand that carried crosses
& their wishing wells weren't watered
with urine, they'd follow
him into river walks.

after his last fall, when the stalks had turned
into sticks, and the last amen had been uttered,

the man they called jesus,
the man i called my father,
would pick up a bottle
of liquor on the way home, point to scabs
on worn paths, slur something about
drifting dreams, and sip and sin
in the name of his
absent father, his
hungry son,
& a holy ghost.

long before i got hurt playing with my
first english word, i used rocks as toys
and juggled juggled them back
and forth, even the jagged ones
that carved into my palms felt
like cotton comforting my
calluses, and even when i missed
& they c-r-a-c-k-e-d into millions
of pieces i'd still feel like
they belonged to me, like
they were natural parts
of my un-bro-ken spa-nish life.

to Papi

& at 6
no alphabets or crayons
to spell letters & draw
curls; you joined your mother
& started selling soap
on streets stained with sweat.

jabón, jabón,
you'd call out into the ears
of passersby who'd smell the lye
& miss the bleached spots
on your arms,
&
while your friends' fingers
made marbles click & clack,
you would use yours to count
pesos & give change back.

& now that i am 6, the son
that you own, & you have
left for the u.s.a. alone,
i wait for a guava tree to
drop a letter saying you have
enough dollars for mami,
yani and me to join you.

until that day,
i will kick the earth's puddles,
scrub away el salvador's spare soil,
rinse myself with drops of mud,
& curse the distance between dirt,
clean water & our blood.

JOSÉ B. GONZÁLEZ

soccer over headstones

i trip over a headstone
with a name etched with fingernails,
a marble goalie blocking me
from the other side of the cemetery
where a woman's arms wrap around another,
mother to mother.

& outside the gates,
fathers who know the score
refuse to look in,
instead they crush the stomachs
of empty beer bottles every time
they hear of loss.

i head the soccer ball
past a cross
& zig-
      zag across the graves
of someone's daughter,
            someone's son,
open up my   stride   as   wide
as   the   mouth   of   the   sky,
& leap
      over
          tombs,
take kicks so hard that mothers
can feel them in their ripped wombs.

our fingers become barbed wire as we snatch
   the railing of the running freight train, grabbing it
like the head of a wild snake
   slithering through our playground,
we chase it, fists up in the air,
   & pull ourselves up, & as its tail
runs away from us,
   we run over the screams of strangers' mothers & fathers
who yell at us to get away lest we be bitten,
   but the barrio has made our hands out of sandpaper,
at seven we can taste it in our thumbs,
   our fingers rip the winds as we swallow & spit air,
& even when Jaime Gómez, barefoot on the tracks,
   misses the railing & his leg is chewed until there is nothing
left but the ends of a rope near his knee,
   we can feel our hands getting rougher
like the skin of a snake that coils itself around a fire.

mami's days

she sews to sew sleeves all day,
adding arms to shirts,
& leaves in the morning
before the first chocolate melts, returns
with stretched arms that hang
as if they've been pulled by their joints,
& even when it seems that the rest
of her body will not catch up to her will,
she still sews to sew so that
in the end we can join papi in the u.s.
& be whole again.

signs of el salvador

Traffic signs in front of Buelita's house
once stood like soldiers,
firing warnings to yield, stop,
and beware of pedestrians.

That was before the war
made them into cryptograms,
shot
    after
shot,
        bomb
                after
        bomb,
                erasing
                letters
that once shouted orders.

All that's left
are signs
with whispered
warnings.

falling

we mostly hear them
in the middle of the night.
Tío Toño tells us they are
        shooting stars.

and when Yani asks why so many
of them sound like gunshots,
silence creeps in & Yani smiles
because the last star to
        fall
        on
        our
        street
made grown men scream
and as long as stars shoot
like that, she says,
it's best that they
stick to twinkling
        on
        and
        off
        safely
        in
        the
        sky,
        where
        no
        one
        can
        hear
        them

fall
like
a
body
slamming
from
evening
into
a
cruel
dawn.

lola's salvadoran pupusa stand

Lola's
Pupusa stand
Survived corn droughts,
Grease fires, El Niño, three marriages,
Five children, two mothers-in-law, cholera,
REFUSED TO MISS A DAY OF WORK,
Melted cheese, refried beans, and ground pork
Barely winced at sounds of rushed footsteps
Laughed at regulars who missed
A meal because of a shotgun
Wound.

finally,
a day so perfect that
this morning's awakening bombs
are overtaken by a woman's wind chimes
of "tamales, tamales."

on the way to the airport
iguanas hang upside down,
even they smile.

along farms and fields
rotten bullet seeds
are overtaken by flowering weeds.

on the side of the highway
a tall Maquilishuat tree gives
birth to premature pink petals
&
inside a plane headed north,
yani & i fly so high
that we can't tell
cornfields from fences;
it's such a perfect
final day.

PART

U.S.

ENGLISH SCREAMS AND
NEW LONDON'S PROMISED DREAMS

chipping ice out of a soccer ball,
i snap bones with every goal,
kick & make coal,
melt snowmen goalies who are scorched
by every torch that skims their carrot-shaped noses

sammy t., my neighbor, only one in my class
who shares jelly beans at snack time,
comes to me with pigskin in his gloved hands,
cuts in front of a corner kick
so quick to ask me to quit,
cracks his knuckles & says
why don't you play football?

i desert my soccer ball on the fallen
needles of a spruce tree (anything not
to be solo me), leave it for dead,
& make sides even.

mostly i block & move aside,
except for when jimmy fro
from crystal avenue fumbles
the ball, & i pick it up and run
toward the end zone.

it's a victory for me
as i look around for someone
to high-five but out of the corner

of my eye, i see sammy t.
forearm up, aiming for my head,
i have no time to step aside.

& before i can ask why,
my lip bursts and reddens like the color
of my favorite jelly beans,
the kind that feel so soft on my lips
on days that i don't exist,
the kind that may harden
in the harsh northern cold,
but still are nothing compared
to the machetes that slice
into campesinos' skulls.

English Words

my mouth agape
their sharpness
i'll use them
i'll stack them
and scrape away

for these english words
could split my tongue,
to build a wall,
on top of each other,
the sounds that

made of stone,
but one by one
one by one,
smooth them
silence me.

It took a Brown Beat

Nor'easter for me

To learn the

meaning of Beselin

That middle name

I carried on my back

Through hallways

& hid under my desk

When José

would have been okay

But Mrs. Sonnone

pulled it out for show & tell

Letting it

loose among middle-schoolers

Who were looking

For a boy named Sue

But found themselves

a long-haired boy with a name

With a strange beat

that rhymed with

Rhymed with

rhymed with

Nothing &

nothing, so

They started

calling me Mrs. Beasley

& when Papi

learned what they called me,

That I had done

nothing to fight back,

He took off his

brown belt,

Snapped it

'gainst the air

Until it

cracked

& cracked

& cracked

& told me

to go back

To the boy

with the longest name,

Grab him

by his neck,

& remind him

the way he had reminded me

That a name

given just before the time of war

Cannot,

cannot,

Cannot,

ever be

Taken back.

Caribbean Fresco in New England

No pure Caribbean tree grows
In my New England backyard
Full of hickories with Puritan bark.

Capes grow here, sowing
Colonials and Frost fences
In Yankee farms never visited
By palms of the tropics,
But subdivided by apples
And Thanksgiving veggies.

Museums of whales,
Watered by fountains
Of Gloucester watches,
Meet museums of witches,
Filled with trials
Of Salem wizards,
But no museums or wintry greenhouses
Hold Caribbean frescoes.

Still lifes of mangoes and guavas,
Uneaten,
> Unrecognized,
> Unsold,
Sit at farmers' markets,
Grown by hungry and nostalgic curators.

Chronic

that cough her speech,
chopping her syllables,
choking (cough) her mid-
                    sentences,

and since she speaks no english,
i accompany her to her new doctor's office
& translate her ex-
                  haling.

as the nurse walks away after taking
her (cough) weight, my mother tells
me about the word describing her condition,
crónica.

its english twin describes her cough, her tos:
chronic.

her cough,
              (cough)
chronic.

& when the doctor's stethoscope listens to her lungs' sobs
and asks about when her cough (cough) began,
she nods toward the window & says,
tell him about the word
crónica.

but as much as i try to in-
                            hale so that the word
can inch its way (cough) out of my mouth,
i refuse to translate it,
because the word also means
chronicle:
her story,
her life,

& i'm still blowing out my candles,
closing my eyes & wishing that this doctor
will be the one who rewrites the beginning
& erases   the moment

when she saw snow falling
for the first time inside the walls
of that factory where cotton fibers
flaked in the air
& started her cough,
                        (her cough)

in the first of many winters
that wouldn't forgive her for taking
(taking) breath, for selling her lungs
for a cup, a cough of minimum wage.

The Thanksgiving of No Más

they said he had hands of stone, his scarred face showed
that he had been pelted with Panamanian rocks as he
trained himself to get out of neighborhoods made of concrete
that had caved in tender spots from man-made earthquakes.

the leather on his skin matched his championship belts, he
was one of us, knew what a man does when the ground snaps,
when the world starts to spin and opens its mouth so wide
and swallows those who can't get themselves to palmed shelters.

my father's friends had stepped into our boxing room to watch
the match, they never wore gloves but they had been boxing
all their lives, it was November and the cold of a new winter
season had started to step and seep into our home.

before the first blow pounded flesh, my father and his friends
passed around a hat and collected their rage as if they were
tossing coins into Sunday's collection box.

each time their man jabbed,
they would say ésa es mía,
until they all claimed credit for
every punch that landed.

then Sugar Ray became a windmill and their Don Quixote
hit nothing but sweaty air, eyes glared as Sugar Ray danced
without music, made a drum out of the hero of Panama,
the avenger of Latin America.

JOSÉ B. GONZÁLEZ

as beer cans sat still, their fighter's swings got slower,
the eighth round arrived as unexpected as a soldier's sudden
invasion, and just as they were expecting a tank to fire off a shot,
a sniper wounded their fighter in the back. instead of running
for cover under attack, my father and his friends watched as the
battle ended with a white flag with the words "no más."

it was an end they could not accept, nobody wept, the house
erupted, ashes burned. they weren't sure what stung more—
seeing Roberto Durán bury his fists
or having to dig up their own—
day after
day,
morning after
morning,
job after
job,
jab after
jab.

mom's box cutter

A Sunday. Don Chele's bakery
Stops selling communion. Truman Street
Traffic is a shallow shell of a bus.

Bible Avenue. Dresses
Sell salvation. Churches
Worship as a parish inhales blessings.

A teenager with a fresh tattoo. Zulma
Walks with her mother. Their fists
Swing into the sky.

The wind. A drift
Pushes my sister's hair. A collision
Makes the three of them one.

A rusty railing. Yani's forehead
Slams into metal. Zulma's mother
Jumps in between fists.

Adult force. Spit
Falls on my sister's face. The ground
Frozen into a memory of pain.

For days. A painting of Jesus
Reflects off Mom's eyes. Wax
Candles burn slowly.

JOSÉ B. GONZÁLEZ

Months go by. On a Friday.
Mom's station wagon
Slows to a halt near Zulma's house.

A stop. Sister and I
Become backseat witnesses. Mom
Attacks the right of a wrong.

A box cutter. Her hand
Aching for contact. Her strikes.
Assault and release revenge.

After sirens. Her handcuffs
Are loosened. That evening's pizza,
Sliced, like pieces of heart.

Dirtied Gauzes

Brings home boxes of medical gauzes
That serve as napkins, so we use them
For wiping ketchup from the sides of our lips,
Soak them in soap and scrub the sink.

Our friends who are used to cockroaches
Crawling on lemonade glasses and climbing
To the tops of popsicle sticks don't think twice
About seeing the gauzes on our table.

Night after night, the gauzes are lined up
At Mami's factory, marked *irregular*,
Sentenced to a fire. But she saves them
And stacks them like wood into her car
So we can scour the floor's stains.

The evening that little brother is born, she
Is putting herself to sleep with dulce de leche
When she feels her water break
Onto our kitchen floor.

"Be sure to clean up," she screams
As the door is about to close, and she looks
Toward Yani and me and a stack of boxes.

At the hospital, the doctor performs
A cesarean section on Mami,
Who is ready to push and push but is too small
To give birth to such a large child
Born with a flan belly.

Dizzied by English words and Spanish screams,
Papi fills out forms and unintentionally gives
Mami's maiden name, Ortiz, to the newborn.

He is not the only one to make
A mistake that night.

Mami screams for hours as if La Llorona
Had come and gone with infants in hand,
While the nurses make hushing sounds
As if all that is needed is a lullaby.

As the sun cracks through her window, her
Screams shatter until a cleaning man,
Short with dusty dark hair, translates
The pain for her and insists that there
IS
SOMETHING
WRONG
WITH
THIS
WOMAN.

The doctor finds that wrong.

Inside Mami's womb,
An abandoned gauze so small that even
After he performs emergency surgery
And traps it in a jar,
Mami is the only one who can tell
That the gauze was stitched together
In a painfully predictable pattern.

Elvis in the Inner City

I was Elvis in the '70s, not swinging hips,
Not wearing suede shoes, but just the same,
In canvas Chuck Taylors with my own svelte moves,
Spinning rap, scratching vinyl to the tunes of
Kurtis Blow, the Sugarhill Gang, Grandmaster Flash
And the hip-hop of the hibity-hip-hip of other
Rappers, making rap mine, rhyming to
The boogie to the boom of the beat, beat, beat.

Mom and Dad's charros, same as Lawrence Welk
Instrumentals were stuff of old country boleros,
But I had my rap, bebop and I'd rap, rap, rap.

The other side of the city, like the flip side of
A one-hit wonder, bopped heads to Van Morrison,
Jim Morrison, and Van Halen, but I couldn't break
A pop to lyrics that weren't about me,
Inner city, inequality, in the record store
I be.

Boom boxes, size of refrigerators, walked up and
Down projects giving concerts for free,
And rap was made for me.

Until I—a lone white square on a checkerboard,
Reciting amidst Blacks of the block—
Froze, could not get my lips to vibrate,
Sync the refrain of the word
"nigger."

I, rockless, rapless,
Without a side A nor a side B,
Stuttered, strutted, struggled,
To find someone who would
Rhyme with me.

When Every Student Was Named Rodney

to Mrs. Quirk

because of you, gum wrappers cuddle up inside my
pockets when there is no trash basket around.

this recess morning you are on the other side of the playground
& your eyes spot a piece of paper
falling from my direction toward sand.

you grab my wrist, pull my arm like a dog leash,
& show me what to do with refuse,
i don't refuse your orders,
but later when Rodney Johnson trips me as
he cuts me in line, you miss how he rips my pants,
when his pen marks an X on my shirt,
you refuse to make the next move,
when he breaks my eyeglasses,
your face turns as if you approve
and when the other students in that class
change their names to Rodney, you
ignore how they cut my Spanish name.

don't know where all the Rodneys will be in a few years,
Mrs. Quirk, but don't worry, Mrs. Quirk, because i put
things away where they belong, Mrs. Quirk,
even store memories in their proper place, Mrs. Quirk,
you have taught me that, Mrs. Quirk,
you have taught me that, Mrs. Quirk.

When Your Father Is the School Janitor

The piss on the toilet seats seeps into the soles of your worn sneakers, stays trapped in your heels, and your feet smack the floor as you walk back and forth between classes.

You don't laugh when the class clown trips over himself in the cafeteria, sends his tray flying into the tiles, a pile of half-eaten hot dogs sliding in ketchup amidst broken dishes.

You can feel the eyes pointed in your direction as the backslapping makes its way around the room, the brooms come out, the high five-ing gets louder, a mop does a clumsy shuffle.

The awful smell of vomit gets inside your throat, but you know better than to release it, so you swallow it as you walk toward the trash bin, standing straight and poised—as the clanking of silverware rises, as if rebelling in anger from being thrown with careless force, forks diving feet first, spoons spinning to the side, knives landing on puddles of milk and water, the piles of plates spilling to the outer edges of counters, crumbs pounding against walls.

After school when the last basketball has stopped bouncing, you see the dirt and dust from the bottoms of high-tops, the sand from snow boots scratching the hardwood, you notice the circle of lovers' crumpled notes around baskets.

As you leave the school, you keep yourself from kicking the soda cans that are leaning against car tires, and step over the candy wraps that sail back and forth crazily on the lawn.

You go to your job at the supermarket where sales fliers lie on top of grocery carts, the plastic bags you've handed off lining the parking lot.

At night, after you've set the table and have sat down to eat, the school janitor sits wearing his green khakis and tee shirt at the dinner table across from you, asking you to pass him a napkin.

As you hand it to him, you notice that his fingernails are clubbed.

You answer his questions about the day, tell him about how one of the guys at school is getting suspended for keeping a hamster in his locker.

He laughs.

Then he tells you about how he'll need your help once a week. At work. He adds that the medicine he brought back from El Salvador isn't helping his breathing, and if you can stop by for an hour or so to help him move a few desks. Maybe sweep.

Yes, you say, as you turn away like you did when that doctor showed you his X-ray, told you about the months to a year, and asked again why he didn't wear his mask all those years when he painted ships for a living.

Yes, you say, you'll help. Because that is all that's left to do when your father is the school janitor. He is, after all, the school janitor. You hear it in the broom's sweeping.

The school janitor.

Only still. Lonely still.

Back and forth.

The school janitor.

Only still. Lonely.

Still.

In Graduate School

Five weeks ago you recited the class syllabus, cleared
Your throat and held up a sign that said your office
Was open at all

Times.

And four weeks ago my hand wasn't raised
Because I was still clapping for you for saying
We could call on you

Anytime.

Then three weeks ago you started making comments
About Spanish-speaking students who take up desk space
And how some of these students were a disappointment this

Year.

Two weeks ago you held your "No Trespassing" sign up,
Returned a paper with a C- that didn't quite make sense to me
And you rejected my request to meet with you if only for a

Moment.

A week ago you told me to reschedule an appointment
And to come back today, but when I knocked on your door,
You said you were very busy and that I must to return in an

Hour.

Two minutes ago, you held up my paper like it was the tail
Of a city rat, you wouldn't let me speak, you wouldn't hear
A syllable of any words of any sentences, not even for a

Minute.

A minute ago I thought of getting up and leaving my books

Behind.

But a second ago I sat back down because twenty years ago
I lived in a house infested with rats that gnawed through bones
As if they were the cancer that was creeping into my father's

Life.

In two hours I'd have to be home to give him his chemo pills, his
Ills were worse than mine; we would have preferred to be living
In the healthy days, but there was no way he would have let me

Return.

To a penniless, pitiless time when we tiptoed barefoot, avoiding
The snaps of traps, stepping on tails of rats, us gnawing at what
Time had brought. I couldn't, wouldn't go

Back.

Tumor Fruit

Did Papi's gardener's hands, clubbed like arthritic limbs
Pick infectious fruits from their stubborn roots?

Or like Newton's apple, did his cancer follow nature's law
With a random fall and squeeze his tender lungs
Because they were ripe for sickening?

Did the asbestos fields at Thames Valley Steel
Harvest Papi's grapefruit tumor, implanting seeds of
Rotten cells that rang like bells in the middle of the night?

Hanging strange like Billie Holliday's fruit, his tumor
Spread its vicious vines and starved seasons' crops,
Took his heart, went after so much more.

Tumor fruit,
Why so greedy?

Like a rabid roaming dog,
You eat more than
You're fed,
But I refuse to be dead.

At the Obituary Interview

I

he asked
where you were born.

you used to say
in a place where food was a finger pointing north
& desperation was a sticklike hand that rubbed
a wife's 9 full-moon belly, a place where the clayed
skin of houses scabbed into a thirsty river
& roofs caved in like hands cupping aged water.

you once asked me
if the school fights made me wish we had stayed
near coffee bean fields.

& even then I should have said that life is not about kicking
outside a womb, but that it's about eyes catching light.

II

he asked
if you belonged to clubs or organizations.

you used to say
that a knock on a door is a knee on the ground
& that when lava tumbles over a neighbor's home,
it's only a matter of time before it seeps under our beds,
& so you wouldn't turn crawling fingers away.

you once asked me
if I minded the long lines at home,

the bathroom waits, the phone ringing for who,
& the cars honking their horns.

& even then I should have said that I knew you
would not let the air I breathed be painted
the color of someone else's smoke.

III

he asked
if we wanted to ask for donations in lieu of flowers.

you used to say
that the flowers on the edges of the city's sidewalks
were from your first job off the plane
& that each time the flowers resurrected
they remembered their first language.

you once asked me
if I was embarrassed by the earth in your fingernails.

& even then I should have said that your outstretched palms
blocked my view of what was on the other side.

IV

the morning of the obituary
I should have said,
they should have read,
you, Father, may not have lived the answer
but in your story,
beginning,
      middle,
           end,
were crumbs of bread that left a trail
of where you gave & where you bled.

PART

Stealing Shakespeare

FLIPPING A PAGE, CONTROLLING RAGE

Stealing Shakespeare

Winking while rubbing his Elizabethan beard
Like an Aladdin lamp ready to grant him a sonnet,
Shakespeare dared me to steal him.

A diamond-shaped face, jewel, staple bible of English,
Smiled, piled high on *Grapes of Wrath*,
Burning on *Fahrenheit 451*, hard cover,
Wrapped in cloth, dared me to steal him.

The principal's rulebook screamed at me that afternoon,
Warning me to principle myself, but the shouts of Caliban,
Trapped inside that tenth-grade classroom boomed,
Made me forget a bandit's doom,
Reminded me that at sixteen, the only
Latino in that college-level course,
The only student whose notebook spoke poor
Working blue-collar Spanish,
'Twas I.

I needed to steal their books.

The Art of Flipping

I'm fifteen and flipping nickels
From one hand
                    To the other.

It's like that when friends jump
Out of their desks and belly flop
Into the shallow ends of empty pools.

Antonio sat in the back row,
Caught selling pot on the corner
Near Tilley Street right before
A book report was due,
Troy used to sit near the window,
Caught jumping the Domino's driver
Delivering near Truman,
And crazy Ken who'd take up
Two desks, one for himself
And the other for his legs,
He wasn't seen again
After he stole a Benz.

So many empty desks for
Target shooters; someone hollers
As chalk crashes against the blackboard,
And dust shrapnel misses me.

My legs can't stay locked,
They want to chase the ghosts,
Who left my classroom graveyard,

They want to write on desks
And mark the tombstones
Of the missing.

I use hieroglyphics to mark
Their stories and gather
Inked sticks to build little men
But they too wind up hanged.
All it takes is one missing letter
And the sticks are damned.

I shuffle my feet
Back
       And
             Forth
As if I'm kicking the water
That is being drained.

But my body just
               Floats.

There's
No tide
      Or wave to wash
Me ashore, but as I look
Toward the board I see
Mr. DePeter's chalked hand.

He's holding a creased book
By someone named
Henry David Thoreau.

On the cover,
A picture of a pond,
And just as my body
Is bracing itself to follow
The dives of former classmates,
Thoreau grabs the back of my shirt,
Drags me near his pond,
And shows me the art
Of
       Flipping
Book
       Pages.

i couldn't for a teenage bully's death

i couldn't for a bully's teen death—
shot in the abdomen three times—
trigger pulled by the hand of a child
who sought the bullet of a gun
to stop the bull's horns from digging deeper into his abdomen.

before he died in the shadows of Victorians on Coit Street
he stole fieldstones from walls—
only to crack them against storm doors—
he stored rocks in his yard so he could pack
them with snow and whirl them toward the heads
of anyone who tried tiptoeing past his apartment—
the giant outline of his cradled body
captured the enormity of his hands.

at 10 he used those hands to shove chests—
the beatings wouldn't rest against running backs—
even then he'd laugh as if he was chasing rabbits—
it was his habit to make the smaller ones cower.

by his 13th, teachers began crouching—
there was one who cried as he walked out
of the principal's office—
it was as if he was offing them 1 by 1.

watching tv with the door locked—
that's where i was when i heard his hands had been stopped—
on the news they showed people with hands over their mouths.

their lips trembled and they spoke about the times, the crimes.

but my fingers, they stayed tight like fists—
i couldn't for this bully's teen death—
not when this would end the thumping on chests—
i couldn't, though i wish my palms would at least rest—
wished his father's bars, his mother's scars,
hadn't turned him, me, us into this.

My words corralled inside the margins
Of a paper that described illegal immigration,
Each sentence tried to follow assignment guidelines.

Research,
The professor had said,
Was to come from published scholars,
Experts who had studied the impact
Of illegal immigration on this nation.

They had uncles named Sam,
While I had one named Eduardo
Who crossed borders
But had never conducted studies.

What was I to do with him?

Without a vita,
Without a visa,
Without immigration papers,
He had become an expert
On how to hire the right coyote,

Having been hog-tied by the Migra
On his first attempt,
He grew eyes on the back of his head
And learned that the trick to running is to sprint
Before a starting pistol makes its first sound.

He   hurdled
      Over the
      U.S.-Mexico
      Border
On his second try
And kept his feet going
Until he could no longer hear a coyote's howl
Or an immigration officer's growl.
As hard as I tried to keep him
From stepping foot on my paper,
It was impossible to block him
From running through the margins.

The day I quoted him, Uncle Eduardo
Took away the job of a published
Researcher who was in this country
Legally,
            I was sure.

As he described the three-week trek
From a bus station in El Salvador
      Crossing
                  The heart of rattling deserts
      To the mouth
      Of Connecticut,
My notes could not catch up with his words,
He
      Shifted
Through memories
As if he was afraid of someone
Snatching them from him.

Stacking my report on
Top
Of
Essays
With
Alien
Titles,
I could see the
C
That would eventually be placed
On my cover page
For allowing my uncle
To trespass the same way I would
The following semester
In Introduction to American Literature
Where I raised my hand
And uttered the lonely word
"But."

In the Company of Books

The revving of engines sent ducks scattering
until couples in beach shorts tossed a potato chip
or scrap of bread near their beaks, children ran
toward ducks as if to accuse them of being seagulls
meant to fly in skies, not walk on land.

Next to the duck pond, Waterford Library's drop-off box
gulped book after book, and high school backpacks
entered and dropped nickels into copy machines,
while children made crafts and listened to stories
in which the good guys always won.

The parking lot between the pond and the library
had become my own private cubicle; far from the madding
patrons and overfed ducks, I'd sit in my car,
miles away from my own city library
that had a direct view of the polished pillars of
the state Supreme Court.

As I sat in my car in the company of Tom Hardy
that day, my hand so close to Tess's, the
cruiser lights poked my rear view mirror, so I
reached in my pocket—slowly—for my wallet.

When the policeman eyed my stereo and asked
for my license, I pulled out my college ID,
abusing it, as his badge grinned and cruiser sighed.

Once he went back to his patrol and his taillights faded away,
I was more determined than ever to finish my story and circle
around this library like a hungry crow who couldn't be trapped,
like a lost crow dangerously close to giving up on scraps.

little brother

I

final time his best friend bled from lead,
i said, little brother, *he chose to*,
he chose to, and i might as well have
gripped the barrel, pointed to little brother's head.

battled me after that. father gone.
what did little brother have to lose? shot after
shot. mixed with booze.

& during his teens he'd drive away
in the truck he inherited.

i'd say to him, *that neighbor. face*
dangles from your mirror. he carried ounces
in bags. he chose to, he chose to.
didn't you see him?

& all that did was push, push me away,
farther away from me. father away from us,
i couldn't be the one to convince little brother
that sometimes we burn our own ashes.
burn our own dust.

me on the street corner like a hustler,
he'd pass me in that truck,
picture of that dead neighbor dangling,
closed windows. strangling.

(i'd remember little brother's thumb
in his mouth. how i used to want to pull it out)

JOSÉ B. GONZÁLEZ

that truck refused one day. greasy hands
squeezed it & pumped it. was time to
junk it. but little brother wouldn't drag
it away. instead he left it in the driveway,
dead neighbor's picture still facing my way.

he bought a new car. more speed.
same mirrors. more racing. in between chasing,
i'd listen to rap and johnny cash. sometimes the songs
would explain my speed. other times
they would justify my little brother's.

others would tell me to breathe youth
& drink to new traditions. easter became
the hunt of new children. little brother
became another. other holidays turned
ordinary. i moved away, the truck stayed
and each time i visited,
that truck wouldn't let me be.

it was like that for two nickels. since
that neighbor's face first dangled. since
i opened up the newspaper,
carried it in my arms like the body
of a dead man. placed it on little brother's feet.
said, said, said.

. . . and all the while, little brother
knocked down cedar trees.
rows of branches would sit
along driveways, tracing
his footsteps.

wish i could say a knock stopped
the clock & joined our hands

on a walk to a city pier
where trout wiggled away &
we giggled until dinnertime.

but that dangling in the driveway,
he chose to, he chose to,
kept the past in sight.

II

the truck was finally towed away,
salvaged piece by piece at some junkyard
where the mirror may have survived.
taken to another twin. or maybe
it was broken into pieces. that would
have been too easy.

it took the blood sale of a home
to wheel that truck out. every now
and then i can see pieces of it
passing by me, or following
so close behind that i'm back
at the block about to grab
a newspaper, my brother's hand
about to grip my words,
our hands about to distance
themselves like they never
held the same rattle.

III

two decades later, as i turn
the day's front page, a snapshot
of a murdered child brings back
the memory of a picture of a little boy

JOSÉ B. GONZÁLEZ

who collected popsicle sticks
& counted his worth in twenty dollar bills.

in it, he smiles toward the sky. Someone,
somewhere, is uttering the right words,
why, why, why?

there is so much that we try
to throw away:
the ashes and dust
that we have created
& tried to blow
                    into the wind
only to see them
in our rearview
                    mirrors.

words like *he chose to, he chose to,*
that we use to eulogize
someone's son,
someone's best friend,
words that dangle and strangle
and mark beginnings
at the same time that they mark
abrupt ends.

IV

little brother, little brother,
maybe i was the one who chose,
who chose to.

little brother, words won't
let me be close to you, but little brother,
can we start all over again?

Sugarcane

The pages begin to settle for the night
With finals coming.
Study room.
Study hour.
My friend and I quiz each other.

The three husky voices in the other corner miss their
Girlfriends of varsity letters
And mumble about the girls at our college,
The one upstairs who likes massages
And her roommate who found a boyfratfriend
And even the one sitting on the other
Side with the dark guy
With glasses and black moustache,
yes, that one, and why is she with him anyway?
Which reminds them of Cristina Torres,
Yes the one who lives in dorm 14
Has a body that can start a bonfire,
They say.

And I have to keep my head from jerking
Toward their table because her curved smile is my
Secret crush, even if she carries her
Books in designer bags,
She reminds me of sugarcane
I dream of sweetness
How her sugar can,
And they awake me
As they moan in agreement
That *she is not bad, not bad*
For a spic,
My secret, silent crush.

JOSÉ B. GONZÁLEZ

Abandoned '74 Mustang

abandoned the '74 Mustang bleeding rust
internal organs muffled, coughed, black
lung diseased, cat-scan X-ray said transplant
would save her, but a scholarship boy,
college sophomore, without auto health
insurance, no coverage under parents' policy,
would not authorize euthanatize the geriatric
classic, traded her for required textbook in Econ 111,
and the worry on my wallet didn't come from where
the next book would come from but that a convalescent
garage in affluent community would adopt,
pay for surgery, drive her back to her curbside roots
one day point a finger toward the ghetto and say
there lives the one who deserted you.

Brown University Librarian Strike

One side of my lungs still carried smoke
From the strike at my father's factory
So I carried my books cautiously
As I walked toward Brown's rock.

Library staff weren't alone
With their rolling messages,
Wages, benefits, justice,
As students in denim uniforms
Marched in unison, a platoon
Of conscripts registering on the spot.

What could they know about the fire
That forms when the metals of
Wages, benefits, and justice,
Are melted together?

I had heard some of these students' comments
In literature classes, professing their love of Dostoyevsky
Without ever having had a key to the underground,
As if walking around Providence's downtown
Was the same as being poverty bound.

I wasn't about to trade in a zero in my poetry seminar
Just so they could feel like heroes for a semester,
So I lifted my legs as if I were stepping over mud,
And I dived into the literary section, the PS call numbers
Reserved for American authors, but on this day
The books, standing shoulder to shoulder,
Seemed to be blocking my path,
Their backs faced me.

JOSÉ B. GONZÁLEZ

On my way to check my books out,
I avoided eye contact with the portrait
Of John D. Rockefeller, but was pulled toward
The image of Edward Inman Page
And a biography of his life,
. . . born a slave
. . . family escaped through Union lines
. . . one of Brown's first two black graduates
. . . Ralph Ellison's grade school principal
. . . pupils thought him a terror, not because
. . . of his punishments but because they
. . . *abhorred the thought of their idol*
knowing of their delinquency.

Those last words, the final link to the chain
Of protestors outside, wrapped around my books
And weighed them down to the point
Where when I cited the books in my presentation
The following week, they felt heavy like the signs
My father, my idol, carried for hours and days
In the hot sun as he tried to melt
Wages, benefits, and justice into one.

Hollow Shells Revisited

I

we were maybe babies
licking then picking guavas off trees,
cousin Chin & me,

we'd climb to the top of rot then sing teases
to our neighbor's wild gallo, who'd get his
revenge at the gloss of dawn, cockadoodledo
us into the outdoors before the first cup
of chuco was sold on the streets,
where we'd spend days slinging rocks

& when streetlights signaled their first round
of warnings, we'd rush to beat the unbuckling
of a belt (or the bristle of a broom), sneak
into the back of a room & pretend that our hours
had been spent at home, waiting for the last bus
to slip past the sun and baptize the night.

every few moons we'd be given away and caught
by a chipped tooth or a scarred sidewalk, mostly
we'd forget our punishments by the next sun—
unless it was a Saturday night, when
we'd get lost in the weekend's offbeat
and walk into a roomful of men
who would gather in Chin's house to talk
Molina, Norton and Ali. they'd
rap revenge in soft blows
and begin sentences with words like
la, la, la, and las, las, las,

JOSÉ B. GONZÁLEZ

condemning the last names
of presidents and the capital's residents
who preached pride but stood
by when the first flag pole fell into a hole.

II

by the time of Ali & Norton II,
I had moved closer to mcintosh trees
to the land of American pies,
and Chin was allowed inside private doors,
becoming a yes man
listening to no-men talk
about la, la, la, & las, las, las.

III

every now & then,
a picture of Chin so thin,
would catch up to me.

the last one came during college
when I was reading textbooks
about the -nomics of -nomics
of how pennies were supposed
to roll so smoothly off dollars.

while our newspapers were reporting
that Ron was doing wrong
by trading weapons for something/someone,
La Prensa published the picture of Chin
at fourteen in a story about his sentence
for hosting guerrilla Saturdays.

IV

for years I wrote essays but not letters,
it wasn't for a lack of ink,
more like the books I read said Chin's chin
had a goatee like Che's,
he seemed to be the kind of radical, they said,
who would kill priests, nuns, Jesuits
just for the injustice of it.

I believed in our government,
not him. after his time, he moved
to the states to an apartment in the Bronx.

relatives said it was small,
like a prison cell. they
told me I had to visit. in time,
I said.

but I'd use my jeep as an excuse
too many miles, a ping in the engine,
I'd tell them I didn't want to get lost
in the New York streets.

I could shake them off
but that photo of him,
I couldn't shake,
couldn't shake that.

V

I have yet to see the graffiti art that (I've been told)
wraps around his apartment's walls. the lines
on bricks claiming that love exists & that Kilroy
lived there. I've train-tripped to NYC to catch

Broadway (42nd Street twice), Jets, Giants, Yankees,
art exhibits, Madison Square Garden, & each time
I've gone I've avoided his part of the Bronx. kept
driving around & around. I've done what I could
to stop hearing the sounds of sentences beginning
with the words la, la, la,
& las, las, las,
done what I could to avoid hearing words
that I should have heard all along,
la,
      la,
            la,
las,
      las,
            las,
la,
      la,
            la,
las,
      las,
            las,

words from childhoods lost,
lost, lost, lost,
lost, lost, lost.

Classrooms

LESSONS IN BROWN

In 1967, San Salvador, El Salvador, fathered my brown,
And so I was born in the capital that salutes
The Pacific, the mother of so many brown rivers,
Lakes, ponds, that held hands with volcanic rocks
That tumbled brown, burned the soil brown,
And browned the country in civil brown turmoil
In the 1970s, when my family left for New England,
Where factories, my mother's sewing machine
And my father's spray paint machine were brown,
And I first attended John Winthrop Elementary School,
A school full of browns, a "separate but equal" type
Of brown that was not El Salvador brown
But a desperate-to-move-out-of-the-projects brown,
And so my parents poured their wages into tuition
For a private middle school classroom
Where I was the only brown, and I was taught to make
My language a more subtle brown, so that by the time I
Attended New London High School, which had shades
Of Puerto Rican brown and tints of Latin American brown
I had shed so much brown that I was accused
Of not being enough brown, but I figured
I knew the roots of my brown and felt comfortable
Enough with my brown, even if I was losing some
Of my Spanish brown, and I continued to lose
It too, not because I wanted to, but because
Most of the brown at the college I attended
Was Republican brown, which spoke a different dialect
Of brown, and by the end of my four years,
My Spanish brown had faded so much that it became
An Anglicized Spanish brown, and I was awarded
The college's excellence in English award,

Which I was pretty sure had never been given
To a graduating brown, and when they said, "this
Year's recipient is José González Brown" I could
Have sworn I saw hundreds of people scrape
Their ears in an attempt to fix whatever
Was making them hear brown, and after graduating,
I figured I'd get a job teaching English, even if
I was brown, but at an interview for an English
Teaching position at a small boarding school,
Headmaster told me that if I was serious about
Getting a job, I'd teach Spanish brown, because
There's such a shortage of Spanish browns,
To which I said, "thank you, headmaster, but
I, I, I'd just assume not teach Spanish brown,"
And when his eyes said, "Thank you, Mr.
Brown, but unless you're willing to teach
Spanish brown, I won't have a job for you,
Mr. Brown," I changed my mind and did
What I had to, even if my first language was no
Longer Spanish brown, and I taught there until one
Brown day in the middle of the school year,
I just had to ask him, "I know you hired me
For something else, but someday can I teach English
Here, even if I am brown?" And his office door
replied, "if you didn't want to teach
Spanish brown, maybe you shouldn't have been brown,"
Which told me it was time for me to leave that master
And get my master's and I decided to attend what else?
Brown University, which was Ivy League brown,
And you want to talk about a different shade of brown?
That was like a culture-shock brown, "Mamihelpme,
Thisisabadnovela, I neverseenthisbefore" kind
Of brown, and there were so many educated,
Liberal browns, I thought that there had been some

Kind of going-out-of-business clearance sale
On diplomas for browns, not that the majority
Was brown, but I just wasn't too used
To associating the college experience
With browns, so even a little bit of brown
Was enough to make me think that colleges
Were turning somewhat brown, and while
At Brown, I student-taught at Providence's Hope
High School, which had many browns, so I
Wanted very badly for my students to recognize
My brown and say if he's at Brown and he's brown,
There's hope for us young browns, but they just
Thought I was Brown University brown, not inner-
City brown, and students couldn't see themselves
In my brown, and so unaccustomed were they to seeing
Any shade of brown in front of their class that they
Thought it was impossible that I could be raised
Brown, but I didn't let that get me too much down,
And when I graduated from Brown, I became a Brown
Brown, a brown squared, a Brown times brown,
Which for some people, teachers even, only meant
That I was Ivy Brown because I am brown, which made me
Want to point to Brown graduates who were Brown
Because their parents or grandparents were Brown,
Making them legacy Browns, Browns cubed, and I
Continued my schooling at the University of Rhode
Island and worked toward my PhD because of,
Not in spite of being brown, and I studied literature
That was brown, because growing up, I had been
Assigned stories like "Young Goodman Brown," but
I had never been assigned a book by a brown author,
Which never made sense to me because I just knew
That in all the years that browns had been in the U.S.,
Even in the part that was brown before the U.S. became

JOSÉ B. GONZÁLEZ

The U.S., browns had to have something to say, even if
It wasn't about being brown, and while I worked
On my brown dissertation, I taught English at Three Rivers
Community College, which had quite a few browns,
So many of whom juggled coursework with family
And jobs and being brown that it was tough for them
To one day say, "I have a college degree even though
I'm brown," which made me appreciate being educated
And being brown and I became ABD, A Brown Doctor,
And probably became URI's first English PhD
Brown, which isn't that big a deal because in higher
Education if you're brown you can lay claim
To being the first this and that as a brown,
And that's why when I tell people that I'm a professor
Of English, every once in a while someone says
Something like, "Dr. Brown, you must teach
A different type of English that has to have
Some kind of brown, maybe you teach second
Language brown English or remedial brown
English, or developmental English for the brown,
Because after all you're brown."
But it matters none to me, master of my own
Brown destiny, because even on the coldest,
Snowiest day in Connecticut, even when it seems
I've been brownbeaten, I can still feel the power
Of my own brown, brown like a brown who beat
The Board of Ed, brown like a brown trunk
Of a brown tree that's been whacked and whacked and
Whacked and whacked until it's become nothing but
A strong, brown wooden frame that holds a brown
Diploma high up in the air, telling the world,
"I'm educated,
And I'm brown."

Says that there is only one reason why a fly would be
      Buzzing around my poetry so what does it matter if
It's open form when none of it is classical, not even
      A rhyme would save it from drowning, written
For the have-nots who have not a reserved parking spot
      On the parking lot for tenured faculty, and besides
There's no sign of the sublime in any line of verse
      That's too free, could at least have half the structure
Of a sonnet, there is no song in it, just a false Latin hum,
      And if that's poetry then let any words that are found
In a promotion application or a help wanted ad enter
      The literary canon, let there be laureates for the mute
And the deaf, let poetry announce its own death.

And I say—

Let that black fly buzz around my words,
      Let that black fly open its wings in its own form,
Let that black fly hatch its larvae in the mouths
      Of the ones who call my poetry slight, and let it zigzag
To the left as they swat to the right, let that black fly ski
      On the back of a snowflake, freeze on a cube of ice,
Stick its tongue out as it melts slowly, fizzling
      In a martini on the rocks before it takes flight,
And let it drone in its own lyrics and spit out epithets
      That sober those who say ethnic poetry is easy to write.

Ago, when I jogged from Eminent Domain
Road, out of that Fort Trumbull
Home with cracked aluminum siding, before
The city started siding with pinstripes
And before pens started signing contracts
To get rid of crabgrass and broadleaf,
I'd let our shepherd-mix loose
Near the train tracks, watch it
Chase whistles, as we'd run together
On the city's crosswalks. Piano keys
Would lead us to tap on Main Street, gallop
Up Coit, and stretch each note. He'd
Take the lead from the horns of buses,
Climb hills like scales rising for an encore,
And step dance while winds retuned power lines,
Bolt over broken beer bottles, and dash past
Abandoned buildings. I'd follow him
In a sprint until my legs ached like
The sore veins and decaying
Livers of dormant homeless dwellers,
Who would push us to go and go and go to,
Away from urban timbers
And into the finish line of the suburbs
Where eight years later,
After helping my mother sign away the deed
(a confession of being a weed),
I'd move into my first single-family home,
Where police sirens would be silenced
Where stars would shoot wildly into the sky,

Where I'd take an evening jog
In my basement and fold my treadmill into a safe,
Hidden corner right next to a window
Where I could see the neighbor's full-breed
Pacing back and forth in his backyard,
Squared off by an electric fence,
And I could see the long,
Guilty distance I had traveled.

Portrait of Mother

Her hands warm tortillas
And paint the kitchen table chairs
With discolored fingers
That are worn from scrubbing the sky.

The flour sticking to her palms
Helps her grip clay as she smooths
The bottom of a flower pot
That clothes a naked lilac.

Her arm skin, a thin canvas
Stretches for life as she
Makes a fist and swings slowly
Toward a bottle of painkillers.

Reborn, she tugs the oxygen tube,
Her umbilical cord,
A leash that keeps her away
From volcanoes of her home.

In her grasp is life, breath,

In
      and
            out
            it goes,
In
      and
            out
            it goes,

Darkening and softening her art.

city mouse chase

that midnight mouse used to serenade
through plaster walls,
used to be awakened
by the te amos of midnight novelas
or the te matos of scorned lovers,

or more likely, the scent
of the evening's rice and beans
would seep through keyholes and door cracks
and tap its back, pointing in my direction.

that mouse followed my tracks from
Federal to Huntington to Thompson Court,
and even to Fort Trumbull.

after college, I swore he'd never find a trace of me.

but last night, in between slipping in a dream
of being in a one-family house
a paradise without nighttime sounds,
a mansion where I'd be the one scratching
a vinyl record track without worrying
about the fall of a crumb,
I heard the walls' poison-ivy scratching,

I made pretend that it had crawled into my imagination,
a part of a montage of clouds
and baseballs floating into planets,
the child of a Nor'easter
having a good laugh. But the traces of my life

(or warnings of my future) started
appearing in sinks and cupboards,
outside of drywalls,
inside my bookshelves, claiming
victory by leaving shreds of verse
in scattered piles.

but the day that the mouse devoured Neruda's lines,
the victory was mine. The letters
scattered, maybe even lost. That mouse
must have laughed when it caught up
to Machu Picchu and erased the heights
leaving a heap of dust. His
weakness was in the dawn, but
my strength is in memory
of spirits. I have studied
their words. I have read
them. I have seen the color
of night when we forget.

A Silent Skid

their bicycle tires trampled through tired dirt roads,
(the kind where leaves aren't raked
& trees aren't trimmed).

my mother & father, proud
that their three kids would have a new home
surrounded by smells of pasture,
walked past the dust spat out by skids,
our city past would be behind us,
they said, as they looked toward a shed
that had the smell of old tobacco.

putting his ear to sparrows, my father pointed
toward the woods. acorns, falling branches,
daredevil squirrels. wasn't like the hood.

the tires continued their circling
as boys behind the wheel who could hardly
reach the top of their handlebars scraped
the driveway with screams aimed our way.

my parents' english, too young to know,
or their past too much to think of skids,
stepped about the house spotting a place
where the print of a brown jesus could be hung.

before we could return to the front door
& face the riders of that dirt road again,
my siblings & i complained about the schools,
how we had heard that their roofs
had missing shingles that would let
in the rains, & their gutters, how
they kept old rainwater that splashed

onto notebooks & backpacks,
how school buses could
skid wildly into snow banks
& how the house deposit,
their hours of overtime should
go back into their pockets.

& though they would have hung a hammock
in that backyard, they returned to new london,
where they bought a 2-family house
on a hill that overlooked empty parking lots,
away from the skids of other kids who rode
rusty bikes on roads that kicked dirt that hurt
& stung the eyes

& at night when they slept & rested,
the circle of wheels that brought them
back to the comforts of city buses
also kicked mold & fungus
out of our new home's walls, into their
bedroom in the basement.

years later, when my siblings
& i carried out their belongings,
& we were longing for acorns, falling branches,
& daredevil squirrels, we could still
hear wheels circling around us, sounding
so close by that it felt like we were the ones
riding our bikes recklessly down narrow dirt roads,
gripping our handlebars so tightly that the only thing
that would have stopped us would have been
the sudden,
   sobering
     silence
       of sparrows.

Calling Her

Haven't gotten soil under my fingernails from typing,
But I've peeled my brain like an overripe plantain, scraping

Away words one at a time, and now that the number I grew up
With, 447-0617, is gone, my fingers move at their own pace

And pull me toward patches, the ones with her fingerprints.
The next person who answers that phone will know nothing

About where it has lived, how in heat waves, beads of sweat fell
Into the cracks of vinyl flooring and poured into the basement,

Flooding lungs and dampening family photos. That person will
Know nothing about how the number moved from two-family to

Two-family home, packed in boxes and trash bags, how it rang
Collect calls from El Salvador, cut off bill collectors who said

"So?" about layoffs, know nothing about how its static stayed
With it everywhere it went. Etched on the tomb of my memories,

The number has tricked my fingers into dialing for a voice that is
Gone and refuses to fade, instead it has shoved its way into calls

Intended for friends, even as I've tried desperately to toss it
Outside my door so it could be carried by winds. Decades back,

Calls for a Rosemary, the woman who used to own that number
Would make me sharpen the blade of my careless young tone

JOSÉ B. GONZÁLEZ

Anytime someone asked for her. The cracks in callers' responses
Suggested that her fingers had tried to hold on to that number as

Long as she could, maybe even dialing 911 as she let it go. Now
That 447-0617 has been passed on again, my fingers want to dig

Old memories out of gardens, touch the soil of old yards where
Leaves sailed on old kiddy pools and then dived onto the hoods

Of teen cars, they want to touch a face and call Rosemary's
Relatives only to say, "I'm sorry. Mine was named Marina."

Dark Cinderella

She picks a book with a cover of a Cinderella with dark skin,
And though I sometimes skim and skip words because
I want her to fall asleep long before moonlight wanes
This time I drag my finger slowly from left to right,
And just when I get to the part where Cinderella rushes
Into midnight, I hear my daughter's words that don't quite fit.

This isn't what Cinderella looks like, she says,
As her head bounces from her pillow,
And I think of someone I know,
A fair-skinned woman named Berta I met at a college fair,
Me with one of my boys from high school on my left
And the other on my right, cut-off tee shirts that showed
Our bi's and tri's, I didn't even bother to take off the sunglasses
Over my eyes as I asked her about degrees.

I wouldn't have blamed her if she had cut me off
And yelled, "next!" But she moved like
She had been there with my friends and me
Those times when degrees of separation
Had tripped us, making us miss steps
That led to missteps on ladders and stairs
And led to cold stares from people
Who skimmed our stories.

I'd go on to attend that college
Where Berta moved behind walls
At night and met with students like me
During the day, listening to our Once Upon a Times,
There were times when she'd hear

JOSÉ B. GONZÁLEZ

About how our skins had been smudged,
And she'd take out an eraser
And rub out whatever she could.

She'd take glass slippers and make
Them fit, and that's why when my daughter
Said that our Cinderella wouldn't look like that,
I thought of Berta, what she'd say,
How she'd grab my daughter's hand
And move it from the left to what's right.

So I closed the book and asked what she meant,
And when she pointed to the princess
And answered that Cinderella wouldn't be wearing a
A dress with lace trim, I felt Berta
Touch my daughter's hand and mine again.

Arizona Sides

I will not let Arizona grab my toe,
Its big finger picking sides,
Eeny, meeny, miny, no.
Will not let my tale
Be dragged and retold
Eeny, meeny, miny, no.
Will not become a Juan Doe.
Arizona will not place a tag on my toe,
Eeny meeny, miny, no.
But my holler will still grow,
In Spanish it will go,
De tin marín de do pingüe
Cucara macara títere fue,
Yo no fui, fue Teté
Pégale pégale que él fue.
Eeny, meeny, miny, no,
Arizona, Arizona,
Let me be,
Arizona, Arizona,
Let free be the finale of me.
Let libertad be the finale de mí.

JOSÉ B. GONZÁLEZ

yesterday as her toes tapped
                              tapped
& stopped
              stopped the soccer ball, she passed
                                        past the reach of
legs that moved like scissors.

i screamed run, run, Cassandra,
RUN,
& tried to will her to hear the pangs of death
the soccer war of 1969,
my mother rock-
ing in her chair tap-
ping my back, wait-
ing for air to rise out
of my chest like a sigh of a goal.

that was the year Honduran troops blasted caps of oil tanks
& the nighttime air became flares of body parts:
i could crawl but couldn't kick a soccer ball
but i could hear my father stomp, run
& run (& then stop to put on his uniform), stomp,

                                                    run
& run (& then stop to douse charred bones).

in between snapping the heads of chickens,
& bragging about the header that turned
the deciding home game in El Salvador's favor,
he would carry tapped
                        tap water through fields,

stopping to reach the mouths of two-year-olds like me,
the ones thirsting for a water's drip,

                                    drip (a sip)
or a touch of an absent father's fingertip.

& yesterday, as a boy with wild hair & the wear
of a child (who wins with cheating grins)
caught up to Cassandra's shins & slide tackled
her from behind, a ref looked down
at his own shoes without whistling & walked
away not listening to my protests. my toes
tightened into knots & then hardened
like heads of hammers, they tapped
down into blades of grass, as if pushing nails
into the palms of the earth.

her feet muddied & her knees scabbed,
she wiped dirt from her lips & pushed
herself back up to chase the ball. i willed
her feet to spell the words of war, to forget forgiveness,
to let the poetry of revenge of soccer warriors
be recited through her kicks,
to wind back her leg like
a slingshot, shoot the moon,
leave a sign that she was there,
to stretch the stitches of scars
& remind everyone of her country's past.

but as her legs pulled her to the other side of the field,
her toes tapped
                    tapped the soccer ball forward into a lazy roll
that wandered with an aimless yawn.

i stood
       stood
              still.
waiting for the tremor that never came.

& after she went through the line of players
who high-fived each other
as if there had been no trip
           tripping, she tapped
                      tapped my back &
walked forward
           toward gulps
                gulps of water,
as if that was all that mattered,
as if it was 1969 & she had been witness
to the sudden disappearance of a father.

Lines Breaking

red pen in hand,
he tells me lines should
                              break
in order to empha-
                    size
certain words
like the ones in my family's history:
first-
        shift
second-
        shift
third-
        shift,

that words are like the earth
            shifting
back and
            forth during an
earth-
        quake
& that verse has more meaning
when words can teeter-
                        totter.

but as much as I try to
break the lines in their proper
                              poetic
                                    places
there are words

that I cannot separate,
like father, mother and child,

words that I cannot break again
like father and leaving, mother and deserting,
child and hurting,

words that stay together all by themselves,
like immigration, isolation, desolation.

José B. González was born in San Salvador, El Salvador, and lived there until the age of eight, at which point he emigrated to the United States and was reunited with his parents, who had left to escape their country's civil turmoil and to find work.

A Fulbright Scholar to Spain, he has been the recipient of such honors as the New England Association of Teachers of English Poet of the Year Award and the American Association of Hispanics in Higher Education Outstanding Latino Faculty of the Year Award. His poetry has appeared in numerous anthologies including *Theatre Under My Skin: Contemporary Salvadoran Poetry* and journals such as *Callaloo, Calabash*, and *Palabra*. A member of the Macondo Writers Workshop, he is the coeditor, with John S. Christie, of *Latino Boom: An Anthology of U.S. Latino Literature*.

A nationally known speaker, González has presented at various colleges such as Harvard University and Cornell University; countries including Mexico, Spain, and El Salvador; and institutions including the Smithsonian Latino Center and the Smithsonian Museum of the American Indian. The founder and editor of LatinoStories.Com, he has been featured in the nationally syndicated show *American Latino TV* and been a contributor to National Public Radio.

Once a non-English speaker, he now has a PhD in English and is a Professor of English at the U.S. Coast Guard Academy in New London, CT. He lives in Quaker Hill, CT, with his wife, three strong daughters, and a son who is starting to believe that being a strong man and standing up for women's rights can go hand in hand.